Bug

JOURNAL

THIS BOOK BELONGS TO:

CONTACT INFORMATION	
NAME:	
ADDRESS:	
PHONE:	

START / END DATES

_____ / ___ / ___   TO   _____ / ___ / ___

BUG JOURNAL

DATE:		TIME:		SEASON:	○ SPRING ○ SUMMER ○ FALL ○ WINTER
WEATHER CONDITIONS:		○ HOT ○ WARM ○ SUNNY ○ CLOUDY ○ RAINY ○ WINDY ○ FOGGY ○ COLD			
BUG NAME:					
WHERE DID YOU FIND IT?					
WHAT COLOR(S) IS THE BUG?					
NUMBER OF LEGS?			DOES IT HAVE WINGS?	○ YES ○ NO ○ NOT SURE	
NUMBER OF LEGS?					
THE BUG IS...		○ BIG ○ SHINY ○ FAST ○ SCARY ○ LITTLE ○ SLOW ○ CUTE ○ ROUND ○ THIN			
DOES IT MAKE ANY SOUND?	○ YES ○ NO		WAS IT ALONE OR IN A GROUP?	○ ALONE ○ GROUP	

NOTES

PHOTO/DRAWING

BUG JOURNAL

DATE:		TIME:		SEASON:	○ SPRING ○ SUMMER ○ FALL ○ WINTER
WEATHER CONDITIONS:		○ HOT ○ WARM ○ SUNNY ○ CLOUDY ○ RAINY ○ WINDY ○ FOGGY ○ COLD			
BUG NAME:					
WHERE DID YOU FIND IT?					
WHAT COLOR(S) IS THE BUG?					
NUMBER OF LEGS?		DOES IT HAVE WINGS?	○ YES ○ NO ○ NOT SURE		
NUMBER OF LEGS?					
THE BUG IS...		○ BIG ○ SHINY ○ FAST ○ SCARY ○ LITTLE ○ SLOW ○ CUTE ○ ROUND ○ THIN			
DOES IT MAKE ANY SOUND?	○ YES ○ NO	WAS IT ALONE OR IN A GROUP?	○ ALONE ○ GROUP		

NOTES

PHOTO/DRAWING

BUG JOURNAL

DATE:		TIME:		SEASON:	○ SPRING ○ SUMMER ○ FALL ○ WINTER
WEATHER CONDITIONS:		○ HOT ○ WARM ○ SUNNY ○ CLOUDY ○ RAINY ○ WINDY ○ FOGGY ○ COLD			
BUG NAME:					
WHERE DID YOU FIND IT?					
WHAT COLOR(S) IS THE BUG?					
NUMBER OF LEGS?			**DOES IT HAVE WINGS?**	○ YES ○ NO ○ NOT SURE	
NUMBER OF LEGS?					
THE BUG IS...		○ BIG ○ SHINY ○ FAST ○ SCARY ○ LITTLE ○ SLOW ○ CUTE ○ ROUND ○ THIN			
DOES IT MAKE ANY SOUND?		○ YES ○ NO	**WAS IT ALONE OR IN A GROUP?**		○ ALONE ○ GROUP

NOTES

PHOTO/DRAWING

BUG JOURNAL

DATE:		TIME:		SEASON:	○ SPRING ○ SUMMER ○ FALL ○ WINTER
WEATHER CONDITIONS:		○ HOT ○ WARM ○ SUNNY ○ CLOUDY ○ RAINY ○ WINDY ○ FOGGY ○ COLD				
BUG NAME:						
WHERE DID YOU FIND IT?						
WHAT COLOR(S) IS THE BUG?						
NUMBER OF LEGS?		**DOES IT HAVE WINGS?**	○ YES ○ NO ○ NOT SURE			
NUMBER OF LEGS?						
THE BUG IS...		○ BIG ○ SHINY ○ FAST ○ SCARY ○ LITTLE ○ SLOW ○ CUTE ○ ROUND ○ THIN				
DOES IT MAKE ANY SOUND?	○ YES ○ NO	**WAS IT ALONE OR IN A GROUP?**	○ ALONE ○ GROUP			

NOTES

PHOTO/DRAWING

BUG JOURNAL

DATE:		TIME:		SEASON:	○ SPRING ○ SUMMER ○ FALL ○ WINTER
WEATHER CONDITIONS:		○ HOT ○ WARM ○ SUNNY ○ CLOUDY ○ RAINY ○ WINDY ○ FOGGY ○ COLD			
BUG NAME:					
WHERE DID YOU FIND IT?					
WHAT COLOR(S) IS THE BUG?					
NUMBER OF LEGS?		DOES IT HAVE WINGS?	○ YES ○ NO ○ NOT SURE		
NUMBER OF LEGS?					
THE BUG IS...		○ BIG ○ SHINY ○ FAST ○ SCARY ○ LITTLE ○ SLOW ○ CUTE ○ ROUND ○ THIN			
DOES IT MAKE ANY SOUND?	○ YES ○ NO	WAS IT ALONE OR IN A GROUP?	○ ALONE ○ GROUP		

NOTES

PHOTO/DRAWING

BUG JOURNAL

DATE:		TIME:		SEASON:	○ SPRING ○ SUMMER ○ FALL ○ WINTER		
WEATHER CONDITIONS:		○ HOT ○ WARM ○ SUNNY ○ CLOUDY ○ RAINY ○ WINDY ○ FOGGY ○ COLD					
BUG NAME:							
WHERE DID YOU FIND IT?							
WHAT COLOR(S) IS THE BUG?							
NUMBER OF LEGS?			DOES IT HAVE WINGS?		○ YES ○ NO ○ NOT SURE		
NUMBER OF LEGS?							
THE BUG IS...		○ BIG ○ SHINY ○ FAST ○ SCARY ○ LITTLE ○ SLOW ○ CUTE ○ ROUND ○ THIN					
DOES IT MAKE ANY SOUND?		○ YES ○ NO	WAS IT ALONE OR IN A GROUP?			○ ALONE ○ GROUP	

NOTES

PHOTO/DRAWING

BUG JOURNAL

DATE:			TIME:		SEASON:	○ SPRING ○ SUMMER ○ FALL ○ WINTER		
WEATHER CONDITIONS:			○ HOT ○ WARM ○ SUNNY ○ CLOUDY ○ RAINY ○ WINDY ○ FOGGY ○ COLD					
BUG NAME:								
WHERE DID YOU FIND IT?								
WHAT COLOR(S) IS THE BUG?								
NUMBER OF LEGS?				DOES IT HAVE WINGS?		○ YES ○ NO ○ NOT SURE		
NUMBER OF LEGS?								
THE BUG IS...			○ BIG ○ SHINY ○ FAST ○ SCARY ○ LITTLE ○ SLOW ○ CUTE ○ ROUND ○ THIN					
DOES IT MAKE ANY SOUND?			○ YES ○ NO		WAS IT ALONE OR IN A GROUP?		○ ALONE ○ GROUP	

NOTES

PHOTO/DRAWING

BUG JOURNAL

DATE:		TIME:		SEASON:	○ SPRING ○ SUMMER ○ FALL ○ WINTER

WEATHER CONDITIONS:	○ HOT ○ WARM ○ SUNNY ○ CLOUDY ○ RAINY ○ WINDY ○ FOGGY ○ COLD
BUG NAME:	
WHERE DID YOU FIND IT?	
WHAT COLOR(S) IS THE BUG?	

NUMBER OF LEGS?		DOES IT HAVE WINGS?	○ YES ○ NO ○ NOT SURE

NUMBER OF LEGS?	
THE BUG IS...	○ BIG ○ SHINY ○ FAST ○ SCARY ○ LITTLE ○ SLOW ○ CUTE ○ ROUND ○ THIN

DOES IT MAKE ANY SOUND?	○ YES ○ NO	WAS IT ALONE OR IN A GROUP?	○ ALONE ○ GROUP

NOTES

PHOTO/DRAWING

BUG JOURNAL

DATE:		TIME:		SEASON:	○ SPRING ○ SUMMER ○ FALL ○ WINTER		
WEATHER CONDITIONS:		○ HOT ○ WARM ○ SUNNY ○ CLOUDY ○ RAINY ○ WINDY ○ FOGGY ○ COLD					
BUG NAME:							
WHERE DID YOU FIND IT?							
WHAT COLOR(S) IS THE BUG?							
NUMBER OF LEGS?			**DOES IT HAVE WINGS?**		○ YES ○ NO ○ NOT SURE		
NUMBER OF LEGS?							
THE BUG IS...		○ BIG ○ SHINY ○ FAST ○ SCARY ○ LITTLE ○ SLOW ○ CUTE ○ ROUND ○ THIN					
DOES IT MAKE ANY SOUND?		○ YES ○ NO	**WAS IT ALONE OR IN A GROUP?**			○ ALONE ○ GROUP	

NOTES

PHOTO/DRAWING

BUG JOURNAL

DATE:		TIME:		SEASON:	○ SPRING ○ SUMMER ○ FALL ○ WINTER
WEATHER CONDITIONS:		○ HOT ○ WARM ○ SUNNY ○ CLOUDY ○ RAINY ○ WINDY ○ FOGGY ○ COLD			
BUG NAME:					
WHERE DID YOU FIND IT?					
WHAT COLOR(S) IS THE BUG?					
NUMBER OF LEGS?		**DOES IT HAVE WINGS?**	○ YES ○ NO ○ NOT SURE		
NUMBER OF LEGS?					
THE BUG IS...		○ BIG ○ SHINY ○ FAST ○ SCARY ○ LITTLE ○ SLOW ○ CUTE ○ ROUND ○ THIN			
DOES IT MAKE ANY SOUND?	○ YES ○ NO	**WAS IT ALONE OR IN A GROUP?**	○ ALONE ○ GROUP		

NOTES

PHOTO/DRAWING

BUG JOURNAL

DATE:		TIME:		SEASON:	○ SPRING ○ SUMMER ○ FALL ○ WINTER
WEATHER CONDITIONS:		○ HOT ○ WARM ○ SUNNY ○ CLOUDY ○ RAINY ○ WINDY ○ FOGGY ○ COLD			
BUG NAME:					
WHERE DID YOU FIND IT?					
WHAT COLOR(S) IS THE BUG?					
NUMBER OF LEGS?			DOES IT HAVE WINGS?	○ YES ○ NO ○ NOT SURE	
NUMBER OF LEGS?					
THE BUG IS...		○ BIG ○ SHINY ○ FAST ○ SCARY ○ LITTLE ○ SLOW ○ CUTE ○ ROUND ○ THIN			
DOES IT MAKE ANY SOUND?	○ YES ○ NO		WAS IT ALONE OR IN A GROUP?		○ ALONE ○ GROUP

NOTES

PHOTO/DRAWING

BUG JOURNAL

DATE:		TIME:		SEASON:	○ SPRING ○ SUMMER ○ FALL ○ WINTER	
WEATHER CONDITIONS:		○ HOT ○ WARM ○ SUNNY ○ CLOUDY ○ RAINY ○ WINDY ○ FOGGY ○ COLD				
BUG NAME:						
WHERE DID YOU FIND IT?						
WHAT COLOR(S) IS THE BUG?						
NUMBER OF LEGS?			DOES IT HAVE WINGS?	○ YES ○ NO ○ NOT SURE		
NUMBER OF LEGS?						
THE BUG IS...		○ BIG ○ SHINY ○ FAST ○ SCARY ○ LITTLE ○ SLOW ○ CUTE ○ ROUND ○ THIN				
DOES IT MAKE ANY SOUND?	○ YES ○ NO		WAS IT ALONE OR IN A GROUP?		○ ALONE ○ GROUP	

NOTES

PHOTO/DRAWING

BUG JOURNAL

DATE:			TIME:		SEASON:	○ SPRING ○ SUMMER ○ FALL ○ WINTER
WEATHER CONDITIONS:			○ HOT ○ WARM ○ SUNNY ○ CLOUDY ○ RAINY ○ WINDY ○ FOGGY ○ COLD			
BUG NAME:						
WHERE DID YOU FIND IT?						
WHAT COLOR(S) IS THE BUG?						
NUMBER OF LEGS?			DOES IT HAVE WINGS?		○ YES ○ NO ○ NOT SURE	
NUMBER OF LEGS?						
THE BUG IS...			○ BIG ○ SHINY ○ FAST ○ SCARY ○ LITTLE ○ SLOW ○ CUTE ○ ROUND ○ THIN			
DOES IT MAKE ANY SOUND?		○ YES ○ NO	WAS IT ALONE OR IN A GROUP?		○ ALONE ○ GROUP	

NOTES

PHOTO/DRAWING

BUG JOURNAL

DATE:		TIME:		SEASON:	○ SPRING ○ SUMMER ○ FALL ○ WINTER
WEATHER CONDITIONS:		○ HOT ○ WARM ○ SUNNY ○ CLOUDY ○ RAINY ○ WINDY ○ FOGGY ○ COLD			
BUG NAME:					
WHERE DID YOU FIND IT?					
WHAT COLOR(S) IS THE BUG?					
NUMBER OF LEGS?		DOES IT HAVE WINGS?	○ YES ○ NO ○ NOT SURE		
NUMBER OF LEGS?					
THE BUG IS...		○ BIG ○ SHINY ○ FAST ○ SCARY ○ LITTLE ○ SLOW ○ CUTE ○ ROUND ○ THIN			
DOES IT MAKE ANY SOUND?	○ YES ○ NO	WAS IT ALONE OR IN A GROUP?	○ ALONE ○ GROUP		

NOTES

PHOTO/DRAWING

BUG JOURNAL

DATE:		TIME:		SEASON:	○ SPRING ○ SUMMER ○ FALL ○ WINTER
WEATHER CONDITIONS:		○ HOT ○ WARM ○ SUNNY ○ CLOUDY ○ RAINY ○ WINDY ○ FOGGY ○ COLD			
BUG NAME:					
WHERE DID YOU FIND IT?					
WHAT COLOR(S) IS THE BUG?					
NUMBER OF LEGS?		DOES IT HAVE WINGS?		○ YES ○ NO ○ NOT SURE	
NUMBER OF LEGS?					
THE BUG IS...		○ BIG ○ SHINY ○ FAST ○ SCARY ○ LITTLE ○ SLOW ○ CUTE ○ ROUND ○ THIN			
DOES IT MAKE ANY SOUND?	○ YES ○ NO	WAS IT ALONE OR IN A GROUP?		○ ALONE ○ GROUP	

NOTES

PHOTO/DRAWING

BUG JOURNAL

DATE:		TIME:		SEASON:	○ SPRING ○ SUMMER ○ FALL ○ WINTER
WEATHER CONDITIONS:		○ HOT ○ WARM ○ SUNNY ○ CLOUDY ○ RAINY ○ WINDY ○ FOGGY ○ COLD			
BUG NAME:					
WHERE DID YOU FIND IT?					
WHAT COLOR(S) IS THE BUG?					
NUMBER OF LEGS?		DOES IT HAVE WINGS?	○ YES ○ NO ○ NOT SURE		
NUMBER OF LEGS?					
THE BUG IS...		○ BIG ○ SHINY ○ FAST ○ SCARY ○ LITTLE ○ SLOW ○ CUTE ○ ROUND ○ THIN			
DOES IT MAKE ANY SOUND?	○ YES ○ NO	WAS IT ALONE OR IN A GROUP?	○ ALONE ○ GROUP		

NOTES

PHOTO/DRAWING

BUG JOURNAL

DATE:			TIME:		SEASON:	○ SPRING ○ SUMMER ○ FALL ○ WINTER		
WEATHER CONDITIONS:		○ HOT ○ WARM ○ SUNNY ○ CLOUDY ○ RAINY ○ WINDY ○ FOGGY ○ COLD						
BUG NAME:								
WHERE DID YOU FIND IT?								
WHAT COLOR(S) IS THE BUG?								
NUMBER OF LEGS?			DOES IT HAVE WINGS?		○ YES ○ NO ○ NOT SURE			
NUMBER OF LEGS?								
THE BUG IS...		○ BIG ○ SHINY ○ FAST ○ SCARY ○ LITTLE ○ SLOW ○ CUTE ○ ROUND ○ THIN						
DOES IT MAKE ANY SOUND?		○ YES ○ NO	WAS IT ALONE OR IN A GROUP?			○ ALONE ○ GROUP		

NOTES

PHOTO/DRAWING

BUG JOURNAL

DATE:		TIME:		SEASON:	○ SPRING ○ SUMMER ○ FALL ○ WINTER
WEATHER CONDITIONS:		○ HOT ○ WARM ○ SUNNY ○ CLOUDY ○ RAINY ○ WINDY ○ FOGGY ○ COLD			
BUG NAME:					
WHERE DID YOU FIND IT?					
WHAT COLOR(S) IS THE BUG?					
NUMBER OF LEGS?		**DOES IT HAVE WINGS?**	○ YES ○ NO ○ NOT SURE		
NUMBER OF LEGS?					
THE BUG IS...		○ BIG ○ SHINY ○ FAST ○ SCARY ○ LITTLE ○ SLOW ○ CUTE ○ ROUND ○ THIN			
DOES IT MAKE ANY SOUND?	○ YES ○ NO	**WAS IT ALONE OR IN A GROUP?**	○ ALONE ○ GROUP		

NOTES

PHOTO/DRAWING

BUG JOURNAL

DATE:		TIME:		SEASON:	○ SPRING ○ SUMMER ○ FALL ○ WINTER

WEATHER CONDITIONS:	○ HOT ○ WARM ○ SUNNY ○ CLOUDY ○ RAINY ○ WINDY ○ FOGGY ○ COLD
BUG NAME:	
WHERE DID YOU FIND IT?	
WHAT COLOR(S) IS THE BUG?	

NUMBER OF LEGS?		DOES IT HAVE WINGS?	○ YES ○ NO ○ NOT SURE

NUMBER OF LEGS?	
THE BUG IS...	○ BIG ○ SHINY ○ FAST ○ SCARY ○ LITTLE ○ SLOW ○ CUTE ○ ROUND ○ THIN

DOES IT MAKE ANY SOUND?	○ YES ○ NO	WAS IT ALONE OR IN A GROUP?	○ ALONE ○ GROUP

NOTES

PHOTO/DRAWING

BUG JOURNAL

DATE:		TIME:		SEASON:	○ SPRING ○ SUMMER ○ FALL ○ WINTER		
WEATHER CONDITIONS:		○ HOT ○ WARM ○ SUNNY ○ CLOUDY ○ RAINY ○ WINDY ○ FOGGY ○ COLD					
BUG NAME:							
WHERE DID YOU FIND IT?							
WHAT COLOR(S) IS THE BUG?							
NUMBER OF LEGS?			DOES IT HAVE WINGS?	○ YES ○ NO ○ NOT SURE			
NUMBER OF LEGS?							
THE BUG IS...		○ BIG ○ SHINY ○ FAST ○ SCARY ○ LITTLE ○ SLOW ○ CUTE ○ ROUND ○ THIN					
DOES IT MAKE ANY SOUND?	○ YES ○ NO		WAS IT ALONE OR IN A GROUP?		○ ALONE ○ GROUP		

NOTES

PHOTO/DRAWING

BUG JOURNAL

DATE:		TIME:		SEASON:	○ SPRING ○ SUMMER ○ FALL ○ WINTER
WEATHER CONDITIONS:		○ HOT ○ WARM ○ SUNNY ○ CLOUDY ○ RAINY ○ WINDY ○ FOGGY ○ COLD			
BUG NAME:					
WHERE DID YOU FIND IT?					
WHAT COLOR(S) IS THE BUG?					
NUMBER OF LEGS?		**DOES IT HAVE WINGS?**		○ YES ○ NO ○ NOT SURE	
NUMBER OF LEGS?					
THE BUG IS...		○ BIG ○ SHINY ○ FAST ○ SCARY ○ LITTLE ○ SLOW ○ CUTE ○ ROUND ○ THIN			
DOES IT MAKE ANY SOUND?		○ YES ○ NO	**WAS IT ALONE OR IN A GROUP?**	○ ALONE ○ GROUP	

NOTES

PHOTO/DRAWING

BUG JOURNAL

DATE:		TIME:		SEASON:	○ SPRING ○ SUMMER ○ FALL ○ WINTER
WEATHER CONDITIONS:		○ HOT ○ WARM ○ SUNNY ○ CLOUDY ○ RAINY ○ WINDY ○ FOGGY ○ COLD			
BUG NAME:					
WHERE DID YOU FIND IT?					
WHAT COLOR(S) IS THE BUG?					
NUMBER OF LEGS?		DOES IT HAVE WINGS?	○ YES ○ NO ○ NOT SURE		
NUMBER OF LEGS?					
THE BUG IS...		○ BIG ○ SHINY ○ FAST ○ SCARY ○ LITTLE ○ SLOW ○ CUTE ○ ROUND ○ THIN			
DOES IT MAKE ANY SOUND?	○ YES ○ NO	WAS IT ALONE OR IN A GROUP?	○ ALONE ○ GROUP		

NOTES

PHOTO/DRAWING

BUG JOURNAL

DATE:		TIME:		SEASON:	○ SPRING ○ SUMMER ○ FALL ○ WINTER

WEATHER CONDITIONS:	○ HOT ○ WARM ○ SUNNY ○ CLOUDY ○ RAINY ○ WINDY ○ FOGGY ○ COLD

BUG NAME:	

WHERE DID YOU FIND IT?	

WHAT COLOR(S) IS THE BUG?	

NUMBER OF LEGS?		DOES IT HAVE WINGS?	○ YES ○ NO ○ NOT SURE

NUMBER OF LEGS?	

THE BUG IS...	○ BIG ○ SHINY ○ FAST ○ SCARY ○ LITTLE ○ SLOW ○ CUTE ○ ROUND ○ THIN

DOES IT MAKE ANY SOUND?	○ YES ○ NO	WAS IT ALONE OR IN A GROUP?	○ ALONE ○ GROUP

NOTES

PHOTO/DRAWING

BUG JOURNAL

DATE:		TIME:		SEASON:	○ SPRING ○ SUMMER ○ FALL ○ WINTER
WEATHER CONDITIONS:		○ HOT ○ WARM ○ SUNNY ○ CLOUDY ○ RAINY ○ WINDY ○ FOGGY ○ COLD			
BUG NAME:					
WHERE DID YOU FIND IT?					
WHAT COLOR(S) IS THE BUG?					
NUMBER OF LEGS?		DOES IT HAVE WINGS?	○ YES ○ NO ○ NOT SURE		
NUMBER OF LEGS?					
THE BUG IS...		○ BIG ○ SHINY ○ FAST ○ SCARY ○ LITTLE ○ SLOW ○ CUTE ○ ROUND ○ THIN			
DOES IT MAKE ANY SOUND?	○ YES ○ NO	WAS IT ALONE OR IN A GROUP?	○ ALONE ○ GROUP		

NOTES

PHOTO/DRAWING

BUG JOURNAL

DATE:		TIME:		SEASON:	○ SPRING ○ SUMMER ○ FALL ○ WINTER
WEATHER CONDITIONS:		○ HOT ○ WARM ○ SUNNY ○ CLOUDY ○ RAINY ○ WINDY ○ FOGGY ○ COLD			
BUG NAME:					
WHERE DID YOU FIND IT?					
WHAT COLOR(S) IS THE BUG?					
NUMBER OF LEGS?		**DOES IT HAVE WINGS?**	○ YES ○ NO ○ NOT SURE		
NUMBER OF LEGS?					
THE BUG IS...		○ BIG ○ SHINY ○ FAST ○ SCARY ○ LITTLE ○ SLOW ○ CUTE ○ ROUND ○ THIN			
DOES IT MAKE ANY SOUND?	○ YES ○ NO	**WAS IT ALONE OR IN A GROUP?**	○ ALONE ○ GROUP		

NOTES

PHOTO/DRAWING

BUG JOURNAL

DATE:		TIME:		SEASON:	○ SPRING ○ SUMMER ○ FALL ○ WINTER
WEATHER CONDITIONS:		○ HOT ○ WARM ○ SUNNY ○ CLOUDY ○ RAINY ○ WINDY ○ FOGGY ○ COLD			
BUG NAME:					
WHERE DID YOU FIND IT?					
WHAT COLOR(S) IS THE BUG?					
NUMBER OF LEGS?		**DOES IT HAVE WINGS?**	○ YES ○ NO ○ NOT SURE		
NUMBER OF LEGS?					
THE BUG IS...		○ BIG ○ SHINY ○ FAST ○ SCARY ○ LITTLE ○ SLOW ○ CUTE ○ ROUND ○ THIN			
DOES IT MAKE ANY SOUND?	○ YES ○ NO	**WAS IT ALONE OR IN A GROUP?**	○ ALONE ○ GROUP		

NOTES

PHOTO/DRAWING

BUG JOURNAL

DATE:		TIME:		SEASON:	○ SPRING ○ SUMMER ○ FALL ○ WINTER

WEATHER CONDITIONS:	○ HOT ○ WARM ○ SUNNY ○ CLOUDY ○ RAINY ○ WINDY ○ FOGGY ○ COLD
BUG NAME:	
WHERE DID YOU FIND IT?	
WHAT COLOR(S) IS THE BUG?	

NUMBER OF LEGS?		DOES IT HAVE WINGS?	○ YES ○ NO ○ NOT SURE

NUMBER OF LEGS?	
THE BUG IS...	○ BIG ○ SHINY ○ FAST ○ SCARY ○ LITTLE ○ SLOW ○ CUTE ○ ROUND ○ THIN

DOES IT MAKE ANY SOUND?	○ YES ○ NO	WAS IT ALONE OR IN A GROUP?	○ ALONE ○ GROUP

NOTES

PHOTO/DRAWING

BUG JOURNAL

DATE:		TIME:		SEASON:	○ SPRING ○ SUMMER ○ FALL ○ WINTER
WEATHER CONDITIONS:		○ HOT ○ WARM ○ SUNNY ○ CLOUDY ○ RAINY ○ WINDY ○ FOGGY ○ COLD			
BUG NAME:					
WHERE DID YOU FIND IT?					
WHAT COLOR(S) IS THE BUG?					
NUMBER OF LEGS?			DOES IT HAVE WINGS?	○ YES ○ NO ○ NOT SURE	
NUMBER OF LEGS?					
THE BUG IS...		○ BIG ○ SHINY ○ FAST ○ SCARY ○ LITTLE ○ SLOW ○ CUTE ○ ROUND ○ THIN			
DOES IT MAKE ANY SOUND?	○ YES ○ NO		WAS IT ALONE OR IN A GROUP?	○ ALONE ○ GROUP	

NOTES

PHOTO/DRAWING

BUG JOURNAL

DATE:		TIME:		SEASON:	○ SPRING ○ SUMMER ○ FALL ○ WINTER
WEATHER CONDITIONS:		○ HOT ○ WARM ○ SUNNY ○ CLOUDY ○ RAINY ○ WINDY ○ FOGGY ○ COLD			
BUG NAME:					
WHERE DID YOU FIND IT?					
WHAT COLOR(S) IS THE BUG?					
NUMBER OF LEGS?		**DOES IT HAVE WINGS?**		○ YES ○ NO ○ NOT SURE	
NUMBER OF LEGS?					
THE BUG IS...		○ BIG ○ SHINY ○ FAST ○ SCARY ○ LITTLE ○ SLOW ○ CUTE ○ ROUND ○ THIN			
DOES IT MAKE ANY SOUND?	○ YES ○ NO	**WAS IT ALONE OR IN A GROUP?**		○ ALONE ○ GROUP	

NOTES

PHOTO/DRAWING

BUG JOURNAL

DATE:		TIME:		SEASON:	○ SPRING ○ SUMMER ○ FALL ○ WINTER

WEATHER CONDITIONS:	○ HOT ○ WARM ○ SUNNY ○ CLOUDY ○ RAINY ○ WINDY ○ FOGGY ○ COLD
BUG NAME:	
WHERE DID YOU FIND IT?	
WHAT COLOR(S) IS THE BUG?	

NUMBER OF LEGS?		DOES IT HAVE WINGS?	○ YES ○ NO ○ NOT SURE

NUMBER OF LEGS?	
THE BUG IS...	○ BIG ○ SHINY ○ FAST ○ SCARY ○ LITTLE ○ SLOW ○ CUTE ○ ROUND ○ THIN

DOES IT MAKE ANY SOUND?	○ YES ○ NO	WAS IT ALONE OR IN A GROUP?	○ ALONE ○ GROUP

NOTES

PHOTO/DRAWING

BUG JOURNAL

DATE:		TIME:		SEASON:	○ SPRING ○ SUMMER ○ FALL ○ WINTER
WEATHER CONDITIONS:		○ HOT ○ WARM ○ SUNNY ○ CLOUDY ○ RAINY ○ WINDY ○ FOGGY ○ COLD			
BUG NAME:					
WHERE DID YOU FIND IT?					
WHAT COLOR(S) IS THE BUG?					
NUMBER OF LEGS?		**DOES IT HAVE WINGS?**	○ YES ○ NO ○ NOT SURE		
NUMBER OF LEGS?					
THE BUG IS.,.	○ BIG ○ SHINY ○ FAST ○ SCARY ○ LITTLE ○ SLOW ○ CUTE ○ ROUND ○ THIN				
DOES IT MAKE ANY SOUND?	○ YES ○ NO	**WAS IT ALONE OR IN A GROUP?**	○ ALONE ○ GROUP		

NOTES

PHOTO/DRAWING

BUG JOURNAL

DATE:		TIME:		SEASON:	○ SPRING ○ SUMMER ○ FALL ○ WINTER
WEATHER CONDITIONS:		○ HOT ○ WARM ○ SUNNY ○ CLOUDY ○ RAINY ○ WINDY ○ FOGGY ○ COLD			
BUG NAME:					
WHERE DID YOU FIND IT?					
WHAT COLOR(S) IS THE BUG?					
NUMBER OF LEGS?		DOES IT HAVE WINGS?	○ YES ○ NO ○ NOT SURE		
NUMBER OF LEGS?					
THE BUG IS...		○ BIG ○ SHINY ○ FAST ○ SCARY ○ LITTLE ○ SLOW ○ CUTE ○ ROUND ○ THIN			
DOES IT MAKE ANY SOUND?	○ YES ○ NO	WAS IT ALONE OR IN A GROUP?	○ ALONE ○ GROUP		

NOTES

PHOTO/DRAWING

BUG JOURNAL

DATE:		TIME:		SEASON:	○ SPRING ○ SUMMER ○ FALL ○ WINTER
WEATHER CONDITIONS:		○ HOT ○ WARM ○ SUNNY ○ CLOUDY ○ RAINY ○ WINDY ○ FOGGY ○ COLD			
BUG NAME:					
WHERE DID YOU FIND IT?					
WHAT COLOR(S) IS THE BUG?					
NUMBER OF LEGS?		**DOES IT HAVE WINGS?**	○ YES ○ NO ○ NOT SURE		
NUMBER OF LEGS?					
THE BUG IS...		○ BIG ○ SHINY ○ FAST ○ SCARY ○ LITTLE ○ SLOW ○ CUTE ○ ROUND ○ THIN			
DOES IT MAKE ANY SOUND?	○ YES ○ NO	**WAS IT ALONE OR IN A GROUP?**	○ ALONE ○ GROUP		

NOTES

PHOTO/DRAWING

BUG JOURNAL

DATE:		**TIME:**	**SEASON:** ○ SPRING ○ SUMMER ○ FALL ○ WINTER

WEATHER CONDITIONS:	○ HOT ○ WARM ○ SUNNY ○ CLOUDY ○ RAINY ○ WINDY ○ FOGGY ○ COLD
BUG NAME:	
WHERE DID YOU FIND IT?	
WHAT COLOR(S) IS THE BUG?	
NUMBER OF LEGS?	**DOES IT HAVE WINGS?** ○ YES ○ NO ○ NOT SURE
NUMBER OF LEGS?	
THE BUG IS...	○ BIG ○ SHINY ○ FAST ○ SCARY ○ LITTLE ○ SLOW ○ CUTE ○ ROUND ○ THIN
DOES IT MAKE ANY SOUND? ○ YES ○ NO	**WAS IT ALONE OR IN A GROUP?** ○ ALONE ○ GROUP

NOTES

PHOTO/DRAWING

BUG JOURNAL

DATE:		TIME:		SEASON:	○ SPRING ○ SUMMER ○ FALL ○ WINTER
WEATHER CONDITIONS:		○ HOT ○ WARM ○ SUNNY ○ CLOUDY ○ RAINY ○ WINDY ○ FOGGY ○ COLD			
BUG NAME:					
WHERE DID YOU FIND IT?					
WHAT COLOR(S) IS THE BUG?					
NUMBER OF LEGS?		**DOES IT HAVE WINGS?**	○ YES ○ NO ○ NOT SURE		
NUMBER OF LEGS?					
THE BUG IS...		○ BIG ○ SHINY ○ FAST ○ SCARY ○ LITTLE ○ SLOW ○ CUTE ○ ROUND ○ THIN			
DOES IT MAKE ANY SOUND?	○ YES ○ NO	**WAS IT ALONE OR IN A GROUP?**		○ ALONE ○ GROUP	

NOTES

PHOTO/DRAWING

BUG JOURNAL

DATE:		TIME:		SEASON:	○ SPRING ○ SUMMER ○ FALL ○ WINTER
WEATHER CONDITIONS:		○ HOT ○ WARM ○ SUNNY ○ CLOUDY ○ RAINY ○ WINDY ○ FOGGY ○ COLD			
BUG NAME:					
WHERE DID YOU FIND IT?					
WHAT COLOR(S) IS THE BUG?					
NUMBER OF LEGS?		**DOES IT HAVE WINGS?**	○ YES ○ NO ○ NOT SURE		
NUMBER OF LEGS?					
THE BUG IS...		○ BIG ○ SHINY ○ FAST ○ SCARY ○ LITTLE ○ SLOW ○ CUTE ○ ROUND ○ THIN			
DOES IT MAKE ANY SOUND?	○ YES ○ NO	**WAS IT ALONE OR IN A GROUP?**	○ ALONE ○ GROUP		

NOTES

PHOTO/DRAWING

BUG JOURNAL

DATE:		TIME:		SEASON:	○ SPRING ○ SUMMER ○ FALL ○ WINTER
WEATHER CONDITIONS:		○ HOT ○ WARM ○ SUNNY ○ CLOUDY ○ RAINY ○ WINDY ○ FOGGY ○ COLD			
BUG NAME:					
WHERE DID YOU FIND IT?					
WHAT COLOR(S) IS THE BUG?					
NUMBER OF LEGS?		**DOES IT HAVE WINGS?**	○ YES ○ NO ○ NOT SURE		
NUMBER OF LEGS?					
THE BUG IS...		○ BIG ○ SHINY ○ FAST ○ SCARY ○ LITTLE ○ SLOW ○ CUTE ○ ROUND ○ THIN			
DOES IT MAKE ANY SOUND?	○ YES ○ NO	**WAS IT ALONE OR IN A GROUP?**	○ ALONE ○ GROUP		

NOTES

PHOTO/DRAWING

BUG JOURNAL

DATE:		TIME:		SEASON:	○ SPRING ○ SUMMER ○ FALL ○ WINTER

WEATHER CONDITIONS:	○ HOT ○ WARM ○ SUNNY ○ CLOUDY ○ RAINY ○ WINDY ○ FOGGY ○ COLD
BUG NAME:	
WHERE DID YOU FIND IT?	
WHAT COLOR(S) IS THE BUG?	

NUMBER OF LEGS?		DOES IT HAVE WINGS?	○ YES ○ NO ○ NOT SURE

NUMBER OF LEGS?	
THE BUG IS...	○ BIG ○ SHINY ○ FAST ○ SCARY ○ LITTLE ○ SLOW ○ CUTE ○ ROUND ○ THIN

DOES IT MAKE ANY SOUND?	○ YES ○ NO	WAS IT ALONE OR IN A GROUP?	○ ALONE ○ GROUP

NOTES

PHOTO/DRAWING

BUG JOURNAL

DATE:		TIME:		SEASON:	○ SPRING ○ SUMMER ○ FALL ○ WINTER
WEATHER CONDITIONS:		○ HOT ○ WARM ○ SUNNY ○ CLOUDY ○ RAINY ○ WINDY ○ FOGGY ○ COLD			
BUG NAME:					
WHERE DID YOU FIND IT?					
WHAT COLOR(S) IS THE BUG?					
NUMBER OF LEGS?		DOES IT HAVE WINGS?		○ YES ○ NO ○ NOT SURE	
NUMBER OF LEGS?					
THE BUG IS...		○ BIG ○ SHINY ○ FAST ○ SCARY ○ LITTLE ○ SLOW ○ CUTE ○ ROUND ○ THIN			
DOES IT MAKE ANY SOUND?	○ YES ○ NO	WAS IT ALONE OR IN A GROUP?		○ ALONE ○ GROUP	

NOTES

PHOTO/DRAWING

BUG JOURNAL

DATE:		TIME:		SEASON:	○ SPRING ○ SUMMER ○ FALL ○ WINTER		
WEATHER CONDITIONS:		○ HOT ○ WARM ○ SUNNY ○ CLOUDY ○ RAINY ○ WINDY ○ FOGGY ○ COLD					
BUG NAME:							
WHERE DID YOU FIND IT?							
WHAT COLOR(S) IS THE BUG?							
NUMBER OF LEGS?			DOES IT HAVE WINGS?		○ YES ○ NO ○ NOT SURE		
NUMBER OF LEGS?							
THE BUG IS...		○ BIG ○ SHINY ○ FAST ○ SCARY ○ LITTLE ○ SLOW ○ CUTE ○ ROUND ○ THIN					
DOES IT MAKE ANY SOUND?		○ YES ○ NO	WAS IT ALONE OR IN A GROUP?		○ ALONE ○ GROUP		

NOTES

PHOTO/DRAWING

BUG JOURNAL

DATE:		TIME:		SEASON:	○ SPRING ○ SUMMER ○ FALL ○ WINTER

WEATHER CONDITIONS:	○ HOT ○ WARM ○ SUNNY ○ CLOUDY ○ RAINY ○ WINDY ○ FOGGY ○ COLD
BUG NAME:	
WHERE DID YOU FIND IT?	
WHAT COLOR(S) IS THE BUG?	

NUMBER OF LEGS?		DOES IT HAVE WINGS?	○ YES ○ NO ○ NOT SURE

NUMBER OF LEGS?	
THE BUG IS...	○ BIG ○ SHINY ○ FAST ○ SCARY ○ LITTLE ○ SLOW ○ CUTE ○ ROUND ○ THIN

DOES IT MAKE ANY SOUND?	○ YES ○ NO	WAS IT ALONE OR IN A GROUP?	○ ALONE ○ GROUP

NOTES

PHOTO/DRAWING

BUG JOURNAL

DATE:		TIME:		SEASON:	○ SPRING ○ SUMMER ○ FALL ○ WINTER		
WEATHER CONDITIONS:		○ HOT ○ WARM ○ SUNNY ○ CLOUDY ○ RAINY ○ WINDY ○ FOGGY ○ COLD					
BUG NAME:							
WHERE DID YOU FIND IT?							
WHAT COLOR(S) IS THE BUG?							
NUMBER OF LEGS?			**DOES IT HAVE WINGS?**		○ YES ○ NO ○ NOT SURE		
NUMBER OF LEGS?							
THE BUG IS...		○ BIG ○ SHINY ○ FAST ○ SCARY ○ LITTLE ○ SLOW ○ CUTE ○ ROUND ○ THIN					
DOES IT MAKE ANY SOUND?		○ YES ○ NO	**WAS IT ALONE OR IN A GROUP?**			○ ALONE ○ GROUP	

NOTES

PHOTO/DRAWING

BUG JOURNAL

DATE:		TIME:		SEASON:	○ SPRING ○ SUMMER ○ FALL ○ WINTER
WEATHER CONDITIONS:		○ HOT ○ WARM ○ SUNNY ○ CLOUDY ○ RAINY ○ WINDY ○ FOGGY ○ COLD			
BUG NAME:					
WHERE DID YOU FIND IT?					
WHAT COLOR(S) IS THE BUG?					
NUMBER OF LEGS?		**DOES IT HAVE WINGS?**	○ YES ○ NO ○ NOT SURE		
NUMBER OF LEGS?					
THE BUG IS...		○ BIG ○ SHINY ○ FAST ○ SCARY ○ LITTLE ○ SLOW ○ CUTE ○ ROUND ○ THIN			
DOES IT MAKE ANY SOUND?	○ YES ○ NO	**WAS IT ALONE OR IN A GROUP?**		○ ALONE ○ GROUP	

NOTES

PHOTO/DRAWING

BUG JOURNAL

DATE:		TIME:		SEASON:	○ SPRING ○ SUMMER ○ FALL ○ WINTER
WEATHER CONDITIONS:		○ HOT ○ WARM ○ SUNNY ○ CLOUDY ○ RAINY ○ WINDY ○ FOGGY ○ COLD			
BUG NAME:					
WHERE DID YOU FIND IT?					
WHAT COLOR(S) IS THE BUG?					
NUMBER OF LEGS?		**DOES IT HAVE WINGS?**	○ YES ○ NO ○ NOT SURE		
NUMBER OF LEGS?					
THE BUG IS...		○ BIG ○ SHINY ○ FAST ○ SCARY ○ LITTLE ○ SLOW ○ CUTE ○ ROUND ○ THIN			
DOES IT MAKE ANY SOUND?	○ YES ○ NO	**WAS IT ALONE OR IN A GROUP?**	○ ALONE ○ GROUP		

NOTES

PHOTO/DRAWING

BUG JOURNAL

DATE:		TIME:		SEASON:	○ SPRING ○ SUMMER ○ FALL ○ WINTER
WEATHER CONDITIONS:		○ HOT ○ WARM ○ SUNNY ○ CLOUDY ○ RAINY ○ WINDY ○ FOGGY ○ COLD			
BUG NAME:					
WHERE DID YOU FIND IT?					
WHAT COLOR(S) IS THE BUG?					
NUMBER OF LEGS?		**DOES IT HAVE WINGS?**	○ YES ○ NO ○ NOT SURE		
NUMBER OF LEGS?					
THE BUG IS...		○ BIG ○ SHINY ○ FAST ○ SCARY ○ LITTLE ○ SLOW ○ CUTE ○ ROUND ○ THIN			
DOES IT MAKE ANY SOUND?	○ YES ○ NO	**WAS IT ALONE OR IN A GROUP?**		○ ALONE ○ GROUP	

NOTES

PHOTO/DRAWING

BUG JOURNAL

DATE:		TIME:		SEASON:	○ SPRING ○ SUMMER ○ FALL ○ WINTER

WEATHER CONDITIONS:	○ HOT ○ WARM ○ SUNNY ○ CLOUDY ○ RAINY ○ WINDY ○ FOGGY ○ COLD
BUG NAME:	
WHERE DID YOU FIND IT?	
WHAT COLOR(S) IS THE BUG?	

NUMBER OF LEGS?		DOES IT HAVE WINGS?	○ YES ○ NO ○ NOT SURE

NUMBER OF LEGS?	
THE BUG IS...	○ BIG ○ SHINY ○ FAST ○ SCARY ○ LITTLE ○ SLOW ○ CUTE ○ ROUND ○ THIN

DOES IT MAKE ANY SOUND?	○ YES ○ NO	WAS IT ALONE OR IN A GROUP?	○ ALONE ○ GROUP

NOTES

PHOTO/DRAWING

BUG JOURNAL

DATE:		TIME:		SEASON:	○ SPRING ○ SUMMER ○ FALL ○ WINTER

WEATHER CONDITIONS:	○ HOT ○ WARM ○ SUNNY ○ CLOUDY ○ RAINY ○ WINDY ○ FOGGY ○ COLD
BUG NAME:	
WHERE DID YOU FIND IT?	
WHAT COLOR(S) IS THE BUG?	

NUMBER OF LEGS?		DOES IT HAVE WINGS?	○ YES ○ NO ○ NOT SURE

NUMBER OF LEGS?	
THE BUG IS...	○ BIG ○ SHINY ○ FAST ○ SCARY ○ LITTLE ○ SLOW ○ CUTE ○ ROUND ○ THIN

DOES IT MAKE ANY SOUND?	○ YES ○ NO	WAS IT ALONE OR IN A GROUP?	○ ALONE ○ GROUP

NOTES

PHOTO/DRAWING

BUG JOURNAL

DATE:		**TIME:**	**SEASON:**	○ SPRING ○ SUMMER ○ FALL ○ WINTER	
WEATHER CONDITIONS:		○ HOT ○ WARM ○ SUNNY ○ CLOUDY ○ RAINY ○ WINDY ○ FOGGY ○ COLD			
BUG NAME:					
WHERE DID YOU FIND IT?					
WHAT COLOR(S) IS THE BUG?					
NUMBER OF LEGS?		**DOES IT HAVE WINGS?**	○ YES ○ NO ○ NOT SURE		
NUMBER OF LEGS?					
THE BUG IS...		○ BIG ○ SHINY ○ FAST ○ SCARY ○ LITTLE ○ SLOW ○ CUTE ○ ROUND ○ THIN			
DOES IT MAKE ANY SOUND?	○ YES ○ NO	**WAS IT ALONE OR IN A GROUP?**	○ ALONE ○ GROUP		

NOTES

PHOTO/DRAWING

BUG JOURNAL

DATE:		TIME:		SEASON:	○ SPRING ○ SUMMER ○ FALL ○ WINTER
WEATHER CONDITIONS:		○ HOT ○ WARM ○ SUNNY ○ CLOUDY ○ RAINY ○ WINDY ○ FOGGY ○ COLD			
BUG NAME:					
WHERE DID YOU FIND IT?					
WHAT COLOR(S) IS THE BUG?					
NUMBER OF LEGS?		**DOES IT HAVE WINGS?**	○ YES ○ NO ○ NOT SURE		
NUMBER OF LEGS?					
THE BUG IS...		○ BIG ○ SHINY ○ FAST ○ SCARY ○ LITTLE ○ SLOW ○ CUTE ○ ROUND ○ THIN			
DOES IT MAKE ANY SOUND?	○ YES ○ NO	**WAS IT ALONE OR IN A GROUP?**		○ ALONE ○ GROUP	

NOTES

PHOTO/DRAWING

BUG JOURNAL

DATE:		TIME:		SEASON:	○ SPRING ○ SUMMER ○ FALL ○ WINTER

WEATHER CONDITIONS:	○ HOT ○ WARM ○ SUNNY ○ CLOUDY ○ RAINY ○ WINDY ○ FOGGY ○ COLD
BUG NAME:	
WHERE DID YOU FIND IT?	
WHAT COLOR(S) IS THE BUG?	

NUMBER OF LEGS?		DOES IT HAVE WINGS?	○ YES ○ NO ○ NOT SURE

NUMBER OF LEGS?	
THE BUG IS...	○ BIG ○ SHINY ○ FAST ○ SCARY ○ LITTLE ○ SLOW ○ CUTE ○ ROUND ○ THIN

DOES IT MAKE ANY SOUND?	○ YES ○ NO	WAS IT ALONE OR IN A GROUP?	○ ALONE ○ GROUP

NOTES

PHOTO/DRAWING

BUG JOURNAL

DATE:		TIME:		SEASON:	○ SPRING ○ SUMMER ○ FALL ○ WINTER
WEATHER CONDITIONS:		○ HOT ○ WARM ○ SUNNY ○ CLOUDY ○ RAINY ○ WINDY ○ FOGGY ○ COLD			
BUG NAME:					
WHERE DID YOU FIND IT?					
WHAT COLOR(S) IS THE BUG?					
NUMBER OF LEGS?		**DOES IT HAVE WINGS?**		○ YES ○ NO ○ NOT SURE	
NUMBER OF LEGS?					
THE BUG IS...		○ BIG ○ SHINY ○ FAST ○ SCARY ○ LITTLE ○ SLOW ○ CUTE ○ ROUND ○ THIN			
DOES IT MAKE ANY SOUND?	○ YES ○ NO	**WAS IT ALONE OR IN A GROUP?**		○ ALONE ○ GROUP	

NOTES

PHOTO/DRAWING

BUG JOURNAL

DATE:		TIME:		SEASON:	○ SPRING ○ SUMMER ○ FALL ○ WINTER		
WEATHER CONDITIONS:		○ HOT ○ WARM ○ SUNNY ○ CLOUDY ○ RAINY ○ WINDY ○ FOGGY ○ COLD					
BUG NAME:							
WHERE DID YOU FIND IT?							
WHAT COLOR(S) IS THE BUG?							
NUMBER OF LEGS?			**DOES IT HAVE WINGS?**		○ YES ○ NO ○ NOT SURE		
NUMBER OF LEGS?							
THE BUG IS...		○ BIG ○ SHINY ○ FAST ○ SCARY ○ LITTLE ○ SLOW ○ CUTE ○ ROUND ○ THIN					
DOES IT MAKE ANY SOUND?		○ YES ○ NO	**WAS IT ALONE OR IN A GROUP?**		○ ALONE ○ GROUP		

NOTES

PHOTO/DRAWING

BUG JOURNAL

DATE:			TIME:		SEASON:	○ SPRING ○ SUMMER ○ FALL ○ WINTER
WEATHER CONDITIONS:			○ HOT ○ WARM ○ SUNNY ○ CLOUDY ○ RAINY ○ WINDY ○ FOGGY ○ COLD			
BUG NAME:						
WHERE DID YOU FIND IT?						
WHAT COLOR(S) IS THE BUG?						
NUMBER OF LEGS?			**DOES IT HAVE WINGS?**	○ YES ○ NO ○ NOT SURE		
NUMBER OF LEGS?						
THE BUG IS...			○ BIG ○ SHINY ○ FAST ○ SCARY ○ LITTLE ○ SLOW ○ CUTE ○ ROUND ○ THIN			
DOES IT MAKE ANY SOUND?		○ YES ○ NO	**WAS IT ALONE OR IN A GROUP?**		○ ALONE ○ GROUP	

NOTES

PHOTO/DRAWING

BUG JOURNAL

DATE:		TIME:		SEASON:	○ SPRING ○ SUMMER ○ FALL ○ WINTER
WEATHER CONDITIONS:		○ HOT ○ WARM ○ SUNNY ○ CLOUDY ○ RAINY ○ WINDY ○ FOGGY ○ COLD			
BUG NAME:					
WHERE DID YOU FIND IT?					
WHAT COLOR(S) IS THE BUG?					
NUMBER OF LEGS?		DOES IT HAVE WINGS?	○ YES ○ NO ○ NOT SURE		
NUMBER OF LEGS?					
THE BUG IS...		○ BIG ○ SHINY ○ FAST ○ SCARY ○ LITTLE ○ SLOW ○ CUTE ○ ROUND ○ THIN			
DOES IT MAKE ANY SOUND?	○ YES ○ NO	WAS IT ALONE OR IN A GROUP?	○ ALONE ○ GROUP		

NOTES

PHOTO/DRAWING

BUG JOURNAL

DATE:		TIME:		SEASON:	○ SPRING ○ SUMMER ○ FALL ○ WINTER
WEATHER CONDITIONS:		○ HOT ○ WARM ○ SUNNY ○ CLOUDY ○ RAINY ○ WINDY ○ FOGGY ○ COLD			
BUG NAME:					
WHERE DID YOU FIND IT?					
WHAT COLOR(S) IS THE BUG?					
NUMBER OF LEGS?		**DOES IT HAVE WINGS?**	○ YES ○ NO ○ NOT SURE		
NUMBER OF LEGS?					
THE BUG IS...		○ BIG ○ SHINY ○ FAST ○ SCARY ○ LITTLE ○ SLOW ○ CUTE ○ ROUND ○ THIN			
DOES IT MAKE ANY SOUND?		○ YES ○ NO	**WAS IT ALONE OR IN A GROUP?**	○ ALONE ○ GROUP	

NOTES

PHOTO/DRAWING

BUG JOURNAL

DATE:		TIME:		SEASON:	○ SPRING ○ SUMMER ○ FALL ○ WINTER
WEATHER CONDITIONS:		○ HOT ○ WARM ○ SUNNY ○ CLOUDY ○ RAINY ○ WINDY ○ FOGGY ○ COLD			
BUG NAME:					
WHERE DID YOU FIND IT?					
WHAT COLOR(S) IS THE BUG?					
NUMBER OF LEGS?		DOES IT HAVE WINGS?	○ YES ○ NO ○ NOT SURE		
NUMBER OF LEGS?					
THE BUG IS...	○ BIG ○ SHINY ○ FAST ○ SCARY ○ LITTLE ○ SLOW ○ CUTE ○ ROUND ○ THIN				
DOES IT MAKE ANY SOUND?	○ YES ○ NO	WAS IT ALONE OR IN A GROUP?	○ ALONE ○ GROUP		

NOTES

PHOTO/DRAWING

BUG JOURNAL

DATE:		TIME:		SEASON:	○ SPRING ○ SUMMER ○ FALL ○ WINTER
WEATHER CONDITIONS:		○ HOT ○ WARM ○ SUNNY ○ CLOUDY ○ RAINY ○ WINDY ○ FOGGY ○ COLD			
BUG NAME:					
WHERE DID YOU FIND IT?					
WHAT COLOR(S) IS THE BUG?					
NUMBER OF LEGS?		**DOES IT HAVE WINGS?**	○ YES ○ NO ○ NOT SURE		
NUMBER OF LEGS?					
THE BUG IS...		○ BIG ○ SHINY ○ FAST ○ SCARY ○ LITTLE ○ SLOW ○ CUTE ○ ROUND ○ THIN			
DOES IT MAKE ANY SOUND?	○ YES ○ NO	**WAS IT ALONE OR IN A GROUP?**	○ ALONE ○ GROUP		

NOTES

PHOTO/DRAWING

BUG JOURNAL

DATE:		TIME:		SEASON:	○ SPRING ○ SUMMER ○ FALL ○ WINTER
WEATHER CONDITIONS:		○ HOT ○ WARM ○ SUNNY ○ CLOUDY ○ RAINY ○ WINDY ○ FOGGY ○ COLD			
BUG NAME:					
WHERE DID YOU FIND IT?					
WHAT COLOR(S) IS THE BUG?					
NUMBER OF LEGS?		**DOES IT HAVE WINGS?**	○ YES ○ NO ○ NOT SURE		
NUMBER OF LEGS?					
THE BUG IS...		○ BIG ○ SHINY ○ FAST ○ SCARY ○ LITTLE ○ SLOW ○ CUTE ○ ROUND ○ THIN			
DOES IT MAKE ANY SOUND?	○ YES ○ NO	**WAS IT ALONE OR IN A GROUP?**	○ ALONE ○ GROUP		

NOTES

PHOTO/DRAWING

BUG JOURNAL

DATE:		TIME:		SEASON:	○ SPRING ○ SUMMER ○ FALL ○ WINTER

WEATHER CONDITIONS:	○ HOT ○ WARM ○ SUNNY ○ CLOUDY ○ RAINY ○ WINDY ○ FOGGY ○ COLD

BUG NAME:	
WHERE DID YOU FIND IT?	
WHAT COLOR(S) IS THE BUG?	

NUMBER OF LEGS?		DOES IT HAVE WINGS?	○ YES ○ NO ○ NOT SURE

NUMBER OF LEGS?	

THE BUG IS...	○ BIG ○ SHINY ○ FAST ○ SCARY ○ LITTLE ○ SLOW ○ CUTE ○ ROUND ○ THIN

DOES IT MAKE ANY SOUND?	○ YES ○ NO	WAS IT ALONE OR IN A GROUP?	○ ALONE ○ GROUP

NOTES

PHOTO/DRAWING

BUG JOURNAL

DATE:		TIME:		SEASON:	○ SPRING ○ SUMMER ○ FALL ○ WINTER
WEATHER CONDITIONS:		○ HOT ○ WARM ○ SUNNY ○ CLOUDY ○ RAINY ○ WINDY ○ FOGGY ○ COLD			
BUG NAME:					
WHERE DID YOU FIND IT?					
WHAT COLOR(S) IS THE BUG?					
NUMBER OF LEGS?		DOES IT HAVE WINGS?	○ YES ○ NO ○ NOT SURE		
NUMBER OF LEGS?					
THE BUG IS...		○ BIG ○ SHINY ○ FAST ○ SCARY ○ LITTLE ○ SLOW ○ CUTE ○ ROUND ○ THIN			
DOES IT MAKE ANY SOUND?	○ YES ○ NO	WAS IT ALONE OR IN A GROUP?		○ ALONE ○ GROUP	

NOTES

PHOTO/DRAWING

BUG JOURNAL

DATE:		TIME:		SEASON:	○ SPRING ○ SUMMER ○ FALL ○ WINTER

WEATHER CONDITIONS:	○ HOT ○ WARM ○ SUNNY ○ CLOUDY ○ RAINY ○ WINDY ○ FOGGY ○ COLD

BUG NAME:	
WHERE DID YOU FIND IT?	
WHAT COLOR(S) IS THE BUG?	

NUMBER OF LEGS?		DOES IT HAVE WINGS?	○ YES ○ NO ○ NOT SURE

NUMBER OF LEGS?	

THE BUG IS...	○ BIG ○ SHINY ○ FAST ○ SCARY ○ LITTLE ○ SLOW ○ CUTE ○ ROUND ○ THIN

DOES IT MAKE ANY SOUND?	○ YES ○ NO	WAS IT ALONE OR IN A GROUP?	○ ALONE ○ GROUP

NOTES

PHOTO/DRAWING

BUG JOURNAL

DATE:		TIME:		SEASON:	SPRING ○ SUMMER ○ FALL ○ WINTER
WEATHER CONDITIONS:		○ HOT ○ WARM ○ SUNNY ○ CLOUDY ○ RAINY ○ WINDY ○ FOGGY ○ COLD			
BUG NAME:					
WHERE DID YOU FIND IT?					
WHAT COLOR(S) IS THE BUG?					
NUMBER OF LEGS?		DOES IT HAVE WINGS?	○ YES ○ NO ○ NOT SURE		
NUMBER OF LEGS?					
THE BUG IS...		○ BIG ○ SHINY ○ FAST ○ SCARY ○ LITTLE ○ SLOW ○ CUTE ○ ROUND ○ THIN			
DOES IT MAKE ANY SOUND?	○ YES ○ NO	WAS IT ALONE OR IN A GROUP?	○ ALONE ○ GROUP		

NOTES

PHOTO/DRAWING

BUG JOURNAL

DATE:		TIME:		SEASON:	○ SPRING ○ SUMMER ○ FALL ○ WINTER
WEATHER CONDITIONS:		○ HOT ○ WARM ○ SUNNY ○ CLOUDY ○ RAINY ○ WINDY ○ FOGGY ○ COLD			
BUG NAME:					
WHERE DID YOU FIND IT?					
WHAT COLOR(S) IS THE BUG?					
NUMBER OF LEGS?		**DOES IT HAVE WINGS?**	○ YES ○ NO ○ NOT SURE		
NUMBER OF LEGS?					
THE BUG IS...		○ BIG ○ SHINY ○ FAST ○ SCARY ○ LITTLE ○ SLOW ○ CUTE ○ ROUND ○ THIN			
DOES IT MAKE ANY SOUND?	○ YES ○ NO	**WAS IT ALONE OR IN A GROUP?**	○ ALONE ○ GROUP		

NOTES

PHOTO/DRAWING

BUG JOURNAL

DATE:		TIME:		SEASON:	○ SPRING ○ SUMMER ○ FALL ○ WINTER		
WEATHER CONDITIONS:		○ HOT ○ WARM ○ SUNNY ○ CLOUDY ○ RAINY ○ WINDY ○ FOGGY ○ COLD					
BUG NAME:							
WHERE DID YOU FIND IT?							
WHAT COLOR(S) IS THE BUG?							
NUMBER OF LEGS?			DOES IT HAVE WINGS?		○ YES ○ NO ○ NOT SURE		
NUMBER OF LEGS?							
THE BUG IS...		○ BIG ○ SHINY ○ FAST ○ SCARY ○ LITTLE ○ SLOW ○ CUTE ○ ROUND ○ THIN					
DOES IT MAKE ANY SOUND?		○ YES ○ NO		WAS IT ALONE OR IN A GROUP?		○ ALONE ○ GROUP	

NOTES

PHOTO/DRAWING

BUG JOURNAL

DATE:		TIME:		SEASON:	○ SPRING ○ SUMMER ○ FALL ○ WINTER

WEATHER CONDITIONS:	○ HOT ○ WARM ○ SUNNY ○ CLOUDY ○ RAINY ○ WINDY ○ FOGGY ○ COLD

BUG NAME:	

WHERE DID YOU FIND IT?	

WHAT COLOR(S) IS THE BUG?	

NUMBER OF LEGS?		DOES IT HAVE WINGS?	○ YES ○ NO ○ NOT SURE

NUMBER OF LEGS?	

THE BUG IS...	○ BIG ○ SHINY ○ FAST ○ SCARY ○ LITTLE ○ SLOW ○ CUTE ○ ROUND ○ THIN

DOES IT MAKE ANY SOUND?	○ YES ○ NO	WAS IT ALONE OR IN A GROUP?	○ ALONE ○ GROUP

NOTES

PHOTO/DRAWING

BUG JOURNAL

DATE:		TIME:		SEASON:	○ SPRING ○ SUMMER ○ FALL ○ WINTER
WEATHER CONDITIONS:		○ HOT ○ WARM ○ SUNNY ○ CLOUDY ○ RAINY ○ WINDY ○ FOGGY ○ COLD			
BUG NAME:					
WHERE DID YOU FIND IT?					
WHAT COLOR(S) IS THE BUG?					
NUMBER OF LEGS?		**DOES IT HAVE WINGS?**	○ YES ○ NO ○ NOT SURE		
NUMBER OF LEGS?					
THE BUG IS...		○ BIG ○ SHINY ○ FAST ○ SCARY ○ LITTLE ○ SLOW ○ CUTE ○ ROUND ○ THIN			
DOES IT MAKE ANY SOUND?	○ YES ○ NO	**WAS IT ALONE OR IN A GROUP?**		○ ALONE ○ GROUP	

NOTES

PHOTO/DRAWING

BUG JOURNAL

DATE:		TIME:		SEASON:	○ SPRING ○ SUMMER ○ FALL ○ WINTER
WEATHER CONDITIONS:		○ HOT ○ WARM ○ SUNNY ○ CLOUDY ○ RAINY ○ WINDY ○ FOGGY ○ COLD			
BUG NAME:					
WHERE DID YOU FIND IT?					
WHAT COLOR(S) IS THE BUG?					
NUMBER OF LEGS?		DOES IT HAVE WINGS?	○ YES ○ NO ○ NOT SURE		
NUMBER OF LEGS?					
THE BUG IS...		○ BIG ○ SHINY ○ FAST ○ SCARY ○ LITTLE ○ SLOW ○ CUTE ○ ROUND ○ THIN			
DOES IT MAKE ANY SOUND?	○ YES ○ NO	WAS IT ALONE OR IN A GROUP?		○ ALONE ○ GROUP	

NOTES

PHOTO/DRAWING

BUG JOURNAL

DATE:		TIME:		SEASON:	○ SPRING ○ SUMMER ○ FALL ○ WINTER	
WEATHER CONDITIONS:		○ HOT ○ WARM ○ SUNNY ○ CLOUDY ○ RAINY ○ WINDY ○ FOGGY ○ COLD				
BUG NAME:						
WHERE DID YOU FIND IT?						
WHAT COLOR(S) IS THE BUG?						
NUMBER OF LEGS?			DOES IT HAVE WINGS?		○ YES ○ NO ○ NOT SURE	
NUMBER OF LEGS?						
THE BUG IS...		○ BIG ○ SHINY ○ FAST ○ SCARY ○ LITTLE ○ SLOW ○ CUTE ○ ROUND ○ THIN				
DOES IT MAKE ANY SOUND?		○ YES ○ NO	WAS IT ALONE OR IN A GROUP?			○ ALONE ○ GROUP

NOTES

PHOTO/DRAWING

BUG JOURNAL

DATE:		TIME:		SEASON:	○ SPRING ○ SUMMER ○ FALL ○ WINTER
WEATHER CONDITIONS:		○ HOT ○ WARM ○ SUNNY ○ CLOUDY ○ RAINY ○ WINDY ○ FOGGY ○ COLD			
BUG NAME:					
WHERE DID YOU FIND IT?					
WHAT COLOR(S) IS THE BUG?					
NUMBER OF LEGS?		**DOES IT HAVE WINGS?**	○ YES ○ NO ○ NOT SURE		
NUMBER OF LEGS?					
THE BUG IS...		○ BIG ○ SHINY ○ FAST ○ SCARY ○ LITTLE ○ SLOW ○ CUTE ○ ROUND ○ THIN			
DOES IT MAKE ANY SOUND?	○ YES ○ NO	**WAS IT ALONE OR IN A GROUP?**	○ ALONE ○ GROUP		

NOTES

PHOTO/DRAWING

BUG JOURNAL

DATE:		TIME:		SEASON:	○ SPRING ○ SUMMER ○ FALL ○ WINTER
WEATHER CONDITIONS:		○ HOT ○ WARM ○ SUNNY ○ CLOUDY ○ RAINY ○ WINDY ○ FOGGY ○ COLD			
BUG NAME:					
WHERE DID YOU FIND IT?					
WHAT COLOR(S) IS THE BUG?					
NUMBER OF LEGS?		**DOES IT HAVE WINGS?**	○ YES ○ NO ○ NOT SURE		
NUMBER OF LEGS?					
THE BUG IS...		○ BIG ○ SHINY ○ FAST ○ SCARY ○ LITTLE ○ SLOW ○ CUTE ○ ROUND ○ THIN			
DOES IT MAKE ANY SOUND?	○ YES ○ NO	**WAS IT ALONE OR IN A GROUP?**	○ ALONE ○ GROUP		

NOTES

PHOTO/DRAWING

BUG JOURNAL

DATE:		TIME:		SEASON:	○ SPRING ○ SUMMER ○ FALL ○ WINTER
WEATHER CONDITIONS:		○ HOT ○ WARM ○ SUNNY ○ CLOUDY ○ RAINY ○ WINDY ○ FOGGY ○ COLD			
BUG NAME:					
WHERE DID YOU FIND IT?					
WHAT COLOR(S) IS THE BUG?					
NUMBER OF LEGS?		**DOES IT HAVE WINGS?**	○ YES ○ NO ○ NOT SURE		
NUMBER OF LEGS?					
THE BUG IS...		○ BIG ○ SHINY ○ FAST ○ SCARY ○ LITTLE ○ SLOW ○ CUTE ○ ROUND ○ THIN			
DOES IT MAKE ANY SOUND?	○ YES ○ NO	**WAS IT ALONE OR IN A GROUP?**	○ ALONE ○ GROUP		

NOTES

PHOTO/DRAWING

BUG JOURNAL

DATE:		**TIME:**	**SEASON:**	○ SPRING ○ SUMMER ○ FALL ○ WINTER

WEATHER CONDITIONS:	○ HOT ○ WARM ○ SUNNY ○ CLOUDY ○ RAINY ○ WINDY ○ FOGGY ○ COLD
BUG NAME:	
WHERE DID YOU FIND IT?	
WHAT COLOR(S) IS THE BUG?	
NUMBER OF LEGS?	**DOES IT HAVE WINGS?** ○ YES ○ NO ○ NOT SURE
NUMBER OF LEGS?	
THE BUG IS...	○ BIG ○ SHINY ○ FAST ○ SCARY ○ LITTLE ○ SLOW ○ CUTE ○ ROUND ○ THIN
DOES IT MAKE ANY SOUND? ○ YES ○ NO	**WAS IT ALONE OR IN A GROUP?** ○ ALONE ○ GROUP

NOTES

PHOTO/DRAWING

BUG JOURNAL

DATE:		TIME:		SEASON:	○ SPRING ○ SUMMER ○ FALL ○ WINTER

WEATHER CONDITIONS:	○ HOT ○ WARM ○ SUNNY ○ CLOUDY ○ RAINY ○ WINDY ○ FOGGY ○ COLD
BUG NAME:	
WHERE DID YOU FIND IT?	
WHAT COLOR(S) IS THE BUG?	

NUMBER OF LEGS?		DOES IT HAVE WINGS?	○ YES ○ NO ○ NOT SURE

NUMBER OF LEGS?	
THE BUG IS...	○ BIG ○ SHINY ○ FAST ○ SCARY ○ LITTLE ○ SLOW ○ CUTE ○ ROUND ○ THIN

DOES IT MAKE ANY SOUND?	○ YES ○ NO	WAS IT ALONE OR IN A GROUP?	○ ALONE ○ GROUP

NOTES

PHOTO/DRAWING

BUG JOURNAL

DATE:		TIME:		SEASON:	○ SPRING ○ SUMMER ○ FALL ○ WINTER
WEATHER CONDITIONS:		○ HOT ○ WARM ○ SUNNY ○ CLOUDY ○ RAINY ○ WINDY ○ FOGGY ○ COLD			
BUG NAME:					
WHERE DID YOU FIND IT?					
WHAT COLOR(S) IS THE BUG?					
NUMBER OF LEGS?		DOES IT HAVE WINGS?		○ YES ○ NO ○ NOT SURE	
NUMBER OF LEGS?					
THE BUG IS...		○ BIG ○ SHINY ○ FAST ○ SCARY ○ LITTLE ○ SLOW ○ CUTE ○ ROUND ○ THIN			
DOES IT MAKE ANY SOUND?	○ YES ○ NO	WAS IT ALONE OR IN A GROUP?		○ ALONE ○ GROUP	

NOTES

PHOTO/DRAWING

BUG JOURNAL

DATE:		TIME:		SEASON:	○ SPRING ○ SUMMER ○ FALL ○ WINTER
WEATHER CONDITIONS:		○ HOT ○ WARM ○ SUNNY ○ CLOUDY ○ RAINY ○ WINDY ○ FOGGY ○ COLD			
BUG NAME:					
WHERE DID YOU FIND IT?					
WHAT COLOR(S) IS THE BUG?					
NUMBER OF LEGS?		DOES IT HAVE WINGS?	○ YES ○ NO ○ NOT SURE		
NUMBER OF LEGS?					
THE BUG IS...		○ BIG ○ SHINY ○ FAST ○ SCARY ○ LITTLE ○ SLOW ○ CUTE ○ ROUND ○ THIN			
DOES IT MAKE ANY SOUND?	○ YES ○ NO	WAS IT ALONE OR IN A GROUP?	○ ALONE ○ GROUP		

NOTES

PHOTO/DRAWING

BUG JOURNAL

DATE:		TIME:		SEASON:	○ SPRING ○ SUMMER ○ FALL ○ WINTER
WEATHER CONDITIONS:		○ HOT ○ WARM ○ SUNNY ○ CLOUDY ○ RAINY ○ WINDY ○ FOGGY ○ COLD			
BUG NAME:					
WHERE DID YOU FIND IT?					
WHAT COLOR(S) IS THE BUG?					
NUMBER OF LEGS?		**DOES IT HAVE WINGS?**	○ YES ○ NO ○ NOT SURE		
NUMBER OF LEGS?					
THE BUG IS...		○ BIG ○ SHINY ○ FAST ○ SCARY ○ LITTLE ○ SLOW ○ CUTE ○ ROUND ○ THIN			
DOES IT MAKE ANY SOUND?	○ YES ○ NO	**WAS IT ALONE OR IN A GROUP?**	○ ALONE ○ GROUP		

NOTES

PHOTO/DRAWING

BUG JOURNAL

DATE:		TIME:		SEASON:	○ SPRING ○ SUMMER ○ FALL ○ WINTER

WEATHER CONDITIONS:	○ HOT ○ WARM ○ SUNNY ○ CLOUDY ○ RAINY ○ WINDY ○ FOGGY ○ COLD

BUG NAME:	

WHERE DID YOU FIND IT?	

WHAT COLOR(S) IS THE BUG?	

NUMBER OF LEGS?		DOES IT HAVE WINGS?	○ YES ○ NO ○ NOT SURE

NUMBER OF LEGS?	

THE BUG IS...	○ BIG ○ SHINY ○ FAST ○ SCARY ○ LITTLE ○ SLOW ○ CUTE ○ ROUND ○ THIN

DOES IT MAKE ANY SOUND?	○ YES ○ NO	WAS IT ALONE OR IN A GROUP?	○ ALONE ○ GROUP

NOTES

PHOTO/DRAWING

BUG JOURNAL

DATE:		TIME:		SEASON:	○ SPRING ○ SUMMER ○ FALL ○ WINTER
WEATHER CONDITIONS:		○ HOT ○ WARM ○ SUNNY ○ CLOUDY ○ RAINY ○ WINDY ○ FOGGY ○ COLD			
BUG NAME:					
WHERE DID YOU FIND IT?					
WHAT COLOR(S) IS THE BUG?					
NUMBER OF LEGS?		**DOES IT HAVE WINGS?**	○ YES ○ NO ○ NOT SURE		
NUMBER OF LEGS?					
THE BUG IS...		○ BIG ○ SHINY ○ FAST ○ SCARY ○ LITTLE ○ SLOW ○ CUTE ○ ROUND ○ THIN			
DOES IT MAKE ANY SOUND?	○ YES ○ NO	**WAS IT ALONE OR IN A GROUP?**		○ ALONE ○ GROUP	

NOTES

PHOTO/DRAWING

BUG JOURNAL

DATE:		TIME:		SEASON:	○ SPRING ○ SUMMER ○ FALL ○ WINTER
WEATHER CONDITIONS:		○ HOT ○ WARM ○ SUNNY ○ CLOUDY ○ RAINY ○ WINDY ○ FOGGY ○ COLD			
BUG NAME:					
WHERE DID YOU FIND IT?					
WHAT COLOR(S) IS THE BUG?					
NUMBER OF LEGS?		DOES IT HAVE WINGS?	○ YES ○ NO ○ NOT SURE		
NUMBER OF LEGS?					
THE BUG IS...	○ BIG ○ SHINY ○ FAST ○ SCARY ○ LITTLE ○ SLOW ○ CUTE ○ ROUND ○ THIN				
DOES IT MAKE ANY SOUND?	○ YES ○ NO	WAS IT ALONE OR IN A GROUP?	○ ALONE ○ GROUP		

NOTES

PHOTO/DRAWING

BUG JOURNAL

DATE:		TIME:		SEASON:	○ SPRING ○ SUMMER ○ FALL ○ WINTER
WEATHER CONDITIONS:		○ HOT ○ WARM ○ SUNNY ○ CLOUDY ○ RAINY ○ WINDY ○ FOGGY ○ COLD			
BUG NAME:					
WHERE DID YOU FIND IT?					
WHAT COLOR(S) IS THE BUG?					
NUMBER OF LEGS?			**DOES IT HAVE WINGS?**	○ YES ○ NO ○ NOT SURE	
NUMBER OF LEGS?					
THE BUG IS...		○ BIG ○ SHINY ○ FAST ○ SCARY ○ LITTLE ○ SLOW ○ CUTE ○ ROUND ○ THIN			
DOES IT MAKE ANY SOUND?	○ YES ○ NO		**WAS IT ALONE OR IN A GROUP?**	○ ALONE ○ GROUP	

NOTES

PHOTO/DRAWING

BUG JOURNAL

DATE:		TIME:		SEASON:	○ SPRING ○ SUMMER ○ FALL ○ WINTER

WEATHER CONDITIONS:	○ HOT ○ WARM ○ SUNNY ○ CLOUDY ○ RAINY ○ WINDY ○ FOGGY ○ COLD
BUG NAME:	
WHERE DID YOU FIND IT?	
WHAT COLOR(S) IS THE BUG?	

NUMBER OF LEGS?		DOES IT HAVE WINGS?	○ YES ○ NO ○ NOT SURE

NUMBER OF LEGS?	
THE BUG IS...	○ BIG ○ SHINY ○ FAST ○ SCARY ○ LITTLE ○ SLOW ○ CUTE ○ ROUND ○ THIN

DOES IT MAKE ANY SOUND?	○ YES ○ NO	WAS IT ALONE OR IN A GROUP?	○ ALONE ○ GROUP

NOTES

PHOTO/DRAWING

BUG JOURNAL

DATE:		TIME:		SEASON:	○ SPRING ○ SUMMER ○ FALL ○ WINTER		
WEATHER CONDITIONS:		○ HOT ○ WARM ○ SUNNY ○ CLOUDY ○ RAINY ○ WINDY ○ FOGGY ○ COLD					
BUG NAME:							
WHERE DID YOU FIND IT?							
WHAT COLOR(S) IS THE BUG?							
NUMBER OF LEGS?			**DOES IT HAVE WINGS?**		○ YES ○ NO ○ NOT SURE		
NUMBER OF LEGS?							
THE BUG IS...		○ BIG ○ SHINY ○ FAST ○ SCARY ○ LITTLE ○ SLOW ○ CUTE ○ ROUND ○ THIN					
DOES IT MAKE ANY SOUND?		○ YES ○ NO	**WAS IT ALONE OR IN A GROUP?**			○ ALONE ○ GROUP	

NOTES

PHOTO/DRAWING

BUG JOURNAL

DATE:		TIME:		SEASON:	○ SPRING ○ SUMMER ○ FALL ○ WINTER
WEATHER CONDITIONS:		○ HOT ○ WARM ○ SUNNY ○ CLOUDY ○ RAINY ○ WINDY ○ FOGGY ○ COLD			
BUG NAME:					
WHERE DID YOU FIND IT?					
WHAT COLOR(S) IS THE BUG?					
NUMBER OF LEGS?		**DOES IT HAVE WINGS?**		○ YES ○ NO ○ NOT SURE	
NUMBER OF LEGS?					
THE BUG IS...		○ BIG ○ SHINY ○ FAST ○ SCARY ○ LITTLE ○ SLOW ○ CUTE ○ ROUND ○ THIN			
DOES IT MAKE ANY SOUND?	○ YES ○ NO	**WAS IT ALONE OR IN A GROUP?**		○ ALONE ○ GROUP	

NOTES

PHOTO/DRAWING

BUG JOURNAL

DATE:		TIME:		SEASON:	○ SPRING ○ SUMMER ○ FALL ○ WINTER
WEATHER CONDITIONS:		○ HOT ○ WARM ○ SUNNY ○ CLOUDY ○ RAINY ○ WINDY ○ FOGGY ○ COLD			
BUG NAME:					
WHERE DID YOU FIND IT?					
WHAT COLOR(S) IS THE BUG?					
NUMBER OF LEGS?		DOES IT HAVE WINGS?	○ YES ○ NO ○ NOT SURE		
NUMBER OF LEGS?					
THE BUG IS...		○ BIG ○ SHINY ○ FAST ○ SCARY ○ LITTLE ○ SLOW ○ CUTE ○ ROUND ○ THIN			
DOES IT MAKE ANY SOUND?	○ YES ○ NO	WAS IT ALONE OR IN A GROUP?	○ ALONE ○ GROUP		

NOTES

PHOTO/DRAWING

BUG JOURNAL

DATE:		TIME:		SEASON:	○ SPRING ○ SUMMER ○ FALL ○ WINTER
WEATHER CONDITIONS:		○ HOT ○ WARM ○ SUNNY ○ CLOUDY ○ RAINY ○ WINDY ○ FOGGY ○ COLD			
BUG NAME:					
WHERE DID YOU FIND IT?					
WHAT COLOR(S) IS THE BUG?					
NUMBER OF LEGS?			**DOES IT HAVE WINGS?**	○ YES ○ NO ○ NOT SURE	
NUMBER OF LEGS?					
THE BUG IS...		○ BIG ○ SHINY ○ FAST ○ SCARY ○ LITTLE ○ SLOW ○ CUTE ○ ROUND ○ THIN			
DOES IT MAKE ANY SOUND?	○ YES ○ NO		**WAS IT ALONE OR IN A GROUP?**	○ ALONE ○ GROUP	

NOTES

PHOTO/DRAWING

BUG JOURNAL

DATE:		TIME:		SEASON:	○ SPRING ○ SUMMER ○ FALL ○ WINTER

WEATHER CONDITIONS:	○ HOT ○ WARM ○ SUNNY ○ CLOUDY ○ RAINY ○ WINDY ○ FOGGY ○ COLD
BUG NAME:	
WHERE DID YOU FIND IT?	
WHAT COLOR(S) IS THE BUG?	

NUMBER OF LEGS?		DOES IT HAVE WINGS?	○ YES ○ NO ○ NOT SURE

NUMBER OF LEGS?	
THE BUG IS...	○ BIG ○ SHINY ○ FAST ○ SCARY ○ LITTLE ○ SLOW ○ CUTE ○ ROUND ○ THIN

DOES IT MAKE ANY SOUND?	○ YES ○ NO	WAS IT ALONE OR IN A GROUP?	○ ALONE ○ GROUP

NOTES

PHOTO/DRAWING

BUG JOURNAL

DATE:		TIME:		SEASON:	○ SPRING ○ SUMMER ○ FALL ○ WINTER

WEATHER CONDITIONS:	○ HOT ○ WARM ○ SUNNY ○ CLOUDY ○ RAINY ○ WINDY ○ FOGGY ○ COLD

BUG NAME:	
WHERE DID YOU FIND IT?	
WHAT COLOR(S) IS THE BUG?	

NUMBER OF LEGS?		DOES IT HAVE WINGS?	○ YES ○ NO ○ NOT SURE

NUMBER OF LEGS?	

THE BUG IS...	○ BIG ○ SHINY ○ FAST ○ SCARY ○ LITTLE ○ SLOW ○ CUTE ○ ROUND ○ THIN

DOES IT MAKE ANY SOUND?	○ YES ○ NO	WAS IT ALONE OR IN A GROUP?	○ ALONE ○ GROUP

NOTES

PHOTO/DRAWING

BUG JOURNAL

DATE:		TIME:		SEASON:	○ SPRING ○ SUMMER ○ FALL ○ WINTER
WEATHER CONDITIONS:		○ HOT ○ WARM ○ SUNNY ○ CLOUDY ○ RAINY ○ WINDY ○ FOGGY ○ COLD			
BUG NAME:					
WHERE DID YOU FIND IT?					
WHAT COLOR(S) IS THE BUG?					
NUMBER OF LEGS?			**DOES IT HAVE WINGS?**	○ YES ○ NO ○ NOT SURE	
NUMBER OF LEGS?					
THE BUG IS...		○ BIG ○ SHINY ○ FAST ○ SCARY ○ LITTLE ○ SLOW ○ CUTE ○ ROUND ○ THIN			
DOES IT MAKE ANY SOUND?	○ YES ○ NO		**WAS IT ALONE OR IN A GROUP?**		○ ALONE ○ GROUP

NOTES

PHOTO/DRAWING

BUG JOURNAL

DATE:		TIME:		SEASON:	○ SPRING ○ SUMMER ○ FALL ○ WINTER
WEATHER CONDITIONS:		○ HOT ○ WARM ○ SUNNY ○ CLOUDY ○ RAINY ○ WINDY ○ FOGGY ○ COLD			
BUG NAME:					
WHERE DID YOU FIND IT?					
WHAT COLOR(S) IS THE BUG?					
NUMBER OF LEGS?		**DOES IT HAVE WINGS?**	○ YES ○ NO ○ NOT SURE		
NUMBER OF LEGS?					
THE BUG IS...		○ BIG ○ SHINY ○ FAST ○ SCARY ○ LITTLE ○ SLOW ○ CUTE ○ ROUND ○ THIN			
DOES IT MAKE ANY SOUND?	○ YES ○ NO	**WAS IT ALONE OR IN A GROUP?**	○ ALONE ○ GROUP		

NOTES

PHOTO/DRAWING

BUG JOURNAL

DATE:		TIME:		SEASON:	○ SPRING ○ SUMMER ○ FALL ○ WINTER

WEATHER CONDITIONS:	○ HOT ○ WARM ○ SUNNY ○ CLOUDY ○ RAINY ○ WINDY ○ FOGGY ○ COLD
BUG NAME:	
WHERE DID YOU FIND IT?	
WHAT COLOR(S) IS THE BUG?	

NUMBER OF LEGS?		DOES IT HAVE WINGS?	○ YES ○ NO ○ NOT SURE

NUMBER OF LEGS?	
THE BUG IS...	○ BIG ○ SHINY ○ FAST ○ SCARY ○ LITTLE ○ SLOW ○ CUTE ○ ROUND ○ THIN

DOES IT MAKE ANY SOUND?	○ YES ○ NO	WAS IT ALONE OR IN A GROUP?	○ ALONE ○ GROUP

NOTES

PHOTO/DRAWING

BUG JOURNAL

DATE:		TIME:		SEASON:	○ SPRING ○ SUMMER ○ FALL ○ WINTER
WEATHER CONDITIONS:		○ HOT ○ WARM ○ SUNNY ○ CLOUDY ○ RAINY ○ WINDY ○ FOGGY ○ COLD			
BUG NAME:					
WHERE DID YOU FIND IT?					
WHAT COLOR(S) IS THE BUG?					
NUMBER OF LEGS?		DOES IT HAVE WINGS?	○ YES ○ NO ○ NOT SURE		
NUMBER OF LEGS?					
THE BUG IS...		○ BIG ○ SHINY ○ FAST ○ SCARY ○ LITTLE ○ SLOW ○ CUTE ○ ROUND ○ THIN			
DOES IT MAKE ANY SOUND?	○ YES ○ NO	WAS IT ALONE OR IN A GROUP?	○ ALONE ○ GROUP		

NOTES

PHOTO/DRAWING

BUG JOURNAL

DATE:		TIME:		SEASON:	○ SPRING ○ SUMMER ○ FALL ○ WINTER
WEATHER CONDITIONS:		○ HOT ○ WARM ○ SUNNY ○ CLOUDY ○ RAINY ○ WINDY ○ FOGGY ○ COLD			
BUG NAME:					
WHERE DID YOU FIND IT?					
WHAT COLOR(S) IS THE BUG?					
NUMBER OF LEGS?			**DOES IT HAVE WINGS?**	○ YES ○ NO ○ NOT SURE	
NUMBER OF LEGS?					
THE BUG IS...		○ BIG ○ SHINY ○ FAST ○ SCARY ○ LITTLE ○ SLOW ○ CUTE ○ ROUND ○ THIN			
DOES IT MAKE ANY SOUND?	○ YES ○ NO		**WAS IT ALONE OR IN A GROUP?**	○ ALONE ○ GROUP	

NOTES

PHOTO/DRAWING

BUG JOURNAL

DATE:		TIME:		SEASON:	○ SPRING ○ SUMMER ○ FALL ○ WINTER
WEATHER CONDITIONS:		○ HOT ○ WARM ○ SUNNY ○ CLOUDY ○ RAINY ○ WINDY ○ FOGGY ○ COLD			
BUG NAME:					
WHERE DID YOU FIND IT?					
WHAT COLOR(S) IS THE BUG?					
NUMBER OF LEGS?		**DOES IT HAVE WINGS?**		○ YES ○ NO ○ NOT SURE	
NUMBER OF LEGS?					
THE BUG IS...		○ BIG ○ SHINY ○ FAST ○ SCARY ○ LITTLE ○ SLOW ○ CUTE ○ ROUND ○ THIN			
DOES IT MAKE ANY SOUND?		○ YES ○ NO	**WAS IT ALONE OR IN A GROUP?**	○ ALONE ○ GROUP	

NOTES

PHOTO/DRAWING

BUG JOURNAL

DATE:		TIME:		SEASON:	○ SPRING ○ SUMMER ○ FALL ○ WINTER
WEATHER CONDITIONS:		○ HOT ○ WARM ○ SUNNY ○ CLOUDY ○ RAINY ○ WINDY ○ FOGGY ○ COLD			
BUG NAME:					
WHERE DID YOU FIND IT?					
WHAT COLOR(S) IS THE BUG?					
NUMBER OF LEGS?		DOES IT HAVE WINGS?		○ YES ○ NO ○ NOT SURE	
NUMBER OF LEGS?					
THE BUG IS...		○ BIG ○ SHINY ○ FAST ○ SCARY ○ LITTLE ○ SLOW ○ CUTE ○ ROUND ○ THIN			
DOES IT MAKE ANY SOUND?	○ YES ○ NO	WAS IT ALONE OR IN A GROUP?		○ ALONE ○ GROUP	

NOTES

PHOTO/DRAWING

BUG JOURNAL

DATE:		TIME:		SEASON:	○ SPRING ○ SUMMER ○ FALL ○ WINTER
WEATHER CONDITIONS:		○ HOT ○ WARM ○ SUNNY ○ CLOUDY ○ RAINY ○ WINDY ○ FOGGY ○ COLD			
BUG NAME:					
WHERE DID YOU FIND IT?					
WHAT COLOR(S) IS THE BUG?					
NUMBER OF LEGS?		DOES IT HAVE WINGS?	○ YES ○ NO ○ NOT SURE		
NUMBER OF LEGS?					
THE BUG IS...		○ BIG ○ SHINY ○ FAST ○ SCARY ○ LITTLE ○ SLOW ○ CUTE ○ ROUND ○ THIN			
DOES IT MAKE ANY SOUND?	○ YES ○ NO	WAS IT ALONE OR IN A GROUP?	○ ALONE ○ GROUP		

NOTES

PHOTO/DRAWING

BUG JOURNAL

DATE:		TIME:		SEASON:	○ SPRING ○ SUMMER ○ FALL ○ WINTER

WEATHER CONDITIONS:	○ HOT ○ WARM ○ SUNNY ○ CLOUDY ○ RAINY ○ WINDY ○ FOGGY ○ COLD

BUG NAME:	

WHERE DID YOU FIND IT?	

WHAT COLOR(S) IS THE BUG?	

NUMBER OF LEGS?		DOES IT HAVE WINGS?	○ YES ○ NO ○ NOT SURE

NUMBER OF LEGS?	

THE BUG IS...	○ BIG ○ SHINY ○ FAST ○ SCARY ○ LITTLE ○ SLOW ○ CUTE ○ ROUND ○ THIN

DOES IT MAKE ANY SOUND?	○ YES ○ NO	WAS IT ALONE OR IN A GROUP?	○ ALONE ○ GROUP

NOTES

PHOTO/DRAWING

BUG JOURNAL

DATE:		TIME:		SEASON:	○ SPRING ○ SUMMER ○ FALL ○ WINTER
WEATHER CONDITIONS:		○ HOT ○ WARM ○ SUNNY ○ CLOUDY ○ RAINY ○ WINDY ○ FOGGY ○ COLD			
BUG NAME:					
WHERE DID YOU FIND IT?					
WHAT COLOR(S) IS THE BUG?					
NUMBER OF LEGS?		**DOES IT HAVE WINGS?**	○ YES ○ NO ○ NOT SURE		
NUMBER OF LEGS?					
THE BUG IS...		○ BIG ○ SHINY ○ FAST ○ SCARY ○ LITTLE ○ SLOW ○ CUTE ○ ROUND ○ THIN			
DOES IT MAKE ANY SOUND?	○ YES ○ NO	**WAS IT ALONE OR IN A GROUP?**	○ ALONE ○ GROUP		

NOTES

PHOTO/DRAWING

BUG JOURNAL

DATE:		TIME:		SEASON:	○ SPRING ○ SUMMER ○ FALL ○ WINTER
WEATHER CONDITIONS:		○ HOT ○ WARM ○ SUNNY ○ CLOUDY ○ RAINY ○ WINDY ○ FOGGY ○ COLD			
BUG NAME:					
WHERE DID YOU FIND IT?					
WHAT COLOR(S) IS THE BUG?					
NUMBER OF LEGS?		DOES IT HAVE WINGS?	○ YES ○ NO ○ NOT SURE		
NUMBER OF LEGS?					
THE BUG IS...		○ BIG ○ SHINY ○ FAST ○ SCARY ○ LITTLE ○ SLOW ○ CUTE ○ ROUND ○ THIN			
DOES IT MAKE ANY SOUND?	○ YES ○ NO	WAS IT ALONE OR IN A GROUP?		○ ALONE ○ GROUP	

NOTES

PHOTO/DRAWING

BUG JOURNAL

DATE:		TIME:		SEASON:	○ SPRING ○ SUMMER ○ FALL ○ WINTER		
WEATHER CONDITIONS:		○ HOT ○ WARM ○ SUNNY ○ CLOUDY ○ RAINY ○ WINDY ○ FOGGY ○ COLD					
BUG NAME:							
WHERE DID YOU FIND IT?							
WHAT COLOR(S) IS THE BUG?							
NUMBER OF LEGS?			DOES IT HAVE WINGS?		○ YES ○ NO ○ NOT SURE		
NUMBER OF LEGS?							
THE BUG IS...		○ BIG ○ SHINY ○ FAST ○ SCARY ○ LITTLE ○ SLOW ○ CUTE ○ ROUND ○ THIN					
DOES IT MAKE ANY SOUND?		○ YES ○ NO		WAS IT ALONE OR IN A GROUP?		○ ALONE ○ GROUP	

NOTES

PHOTO/DRAWING

BUG JOURNAL

DATE:		TIME:		SEASON:	○ SPRING ○ SUMMER ○ FALL ○ WINTER
WEATHER CONDITIONS:		○ HOT ○ WARM ○ SUNNY ○ CLOUDY ○ RAINY ○ WINDY ○ FOGGY ○ COLD			
BUG NAME:					
WHERE DID YOU FIND IT?					
WHAT COLOR(S) IS THE BUG?					
NUMBER OF LEGS?		DOES IT HAVE WINGS?		○ YES ○ NO ○ NOT SURE	
NUMBER OF LEGS?					
THE BUG IS...		○ BIG ○ SHINY ○ FAST ○ SCARY ○ LITTLE ○ SLOW ○ CUTE ○ ROUND ○ THIN			
DOES IT MAKE ANY SOUND?	○ YES ○ NO	WAS IT ALONE OR IN A GROUP?		○ ALONE ○ GROUP	

NOTES

PHOTO/DRAWING

BUG JOURNAL

DATE:		TIME:		SEASON:	○ SPRING ○ SUMMER ○ FALL ○ WINTER

WEATHER CONDITIONS:	○ HOT ○ WARM ○ SUNNY ○ CLOUDY ○ RAINY ○ WINDY ○ FOGGY ○ COLD
BUG NAME:	
WHERE DID YOU FIND IT?	
WHAT COLOR(S) IS THE BUG?	

NUMBER OF LEGS?		DOES IT HAVE WINGS?	○ YES ○ NO ○ NOT SURE

NUMBER OF LEGS?	
THE BUG IS...	○ BIG ○ SHINY ○ FAST ○ SCARY ○ LITTLE ○ SLOW ○ CUTE ○ ROUND ○ THIN

DOES IT MAKE ANY SOUND?	○ YES ○ NO	WAS IT ALONE OR IN A GROUP?	○ ALONE ○ GROUP

NOTES

PHOTO/DRAWING

BUG JOURNAL

DATE:		TIME:		SEASON:	○ SPRING ○ SUMMER ○ FALL ○ WINTER
WEATHER CONDITIONS:		○ HOT ○ WARM ○ SUNNY ○ CLOUDY ○ RAINY ○ WINDY ○ FOGGY ○ COLD			
BUG NAME:					
WHERE DID YOU FIND IT?					
WHAT COLOR(S) IS THE BUG?					
NUMBER OF LEGS?			DOES IT HAVE WINGS?	○ YES ○ NO ○ NOT SURE	
NUMBER OF LEGS?					
THE BUG IS...		○ BIG ○ SHINY ○ FAST ○ SCARY ○ LITTLE ○ SLOW ○ CUTE ○ ROUND ○ THIN			
DOES IT MAKE ANY SOUND?	○ YES ○ NO		WAS IT ALONE OR IN A GROUP?		○ ALONE ○ GROUP

NOTES

PHOTO/DRAWING

BUG JOURNAL

DATE:		TIME:		SEASON:	○ SPRING ○ SUMMER ○ FALL ○ WINTER
WEATHER CONDITIONS:		○ HOT ○ WARM ○ SUNNY ○ CLOUDY ○ RAINY ○ WINDY ○ FOGGY ○ COLD			
BUG NAME:					
WHERE DID YOU FIND IT?					
WHAT COLOR(S) IS THE BUG?					
NUMBER OF LEGS?		DOES IT HAVE WINGS?	○ YES ○ NO ○ NOT SURE		
NUMBER OF LEGS?					
THE BUG IS...		○ BIG ○ SHINY ○ FAST ○ SCARY ○ LITTLE ○ SLOW ○ CUTE ○ ROUND ○ THIN			
DOES IT MAKE ANY SOUND?	○ YES ○ NO	WAS IT ALONE OR IN A GROUP?	○ ALONE ○ GROUP		

NOTES

PHOTO/DRAWING

BUG JOURNAL

DATE:		TIME:		SEASON:	○ SPRING ○ SUMMER ○ FALL ○ WINTER
WEATHER CONDITIONS:		○ HOT ○ WARM ○ SUNNY ○ CLOUDY ○ RAINY ○ WINDY ○ FOGGY ○ COLD			
BUG NAME:					
WHERE DID YOU FIND IT?					
WHAT COLOR(S) IS THE BUG?					
NUMBER OF LEGS?		DOES IT HAVE WINGS?	○ YES ○ NO ○ NOT SURE		
NUMBER OF LEGS?					
THE BUG IS...		○ BIG ○ SHINY ○ FAST ○ SCARY ○ LITTLE ○ SLOW ○ CUTE ○ ROUND ○ THIN			
DOES IT MAKE ANY SOUND?	○ YES ○ NO	WAS IT ALONE OR IN A GROUP?		○ ALONE ○ GROUP	

NOTES

PHOTO/DRAWING

Printed in Great Britain
by Amazon

34745922R00059